Crypto Exchanges from Taiwan

Table of Contents

Chapter 1: Introduction

Chapter 2: Taiwan Crypto Facts 2018

    2.1 Blockchain Bandwagon by Taiwan

    2.2 Asia Blockchain Summit

    2.3 Legitimacy is Increasing the Prices of Digital Currency

    2.4 Cryptocurrency Regulations in Taiwan

    2.5 Taiwan Moves toward Relaxing Cryptocurrency Because of the Constrict Rules in other Countries of Asia

    2.6 People were Hesitant in the Past

    2.7 Regulatory Narrowing Overseas

    2.8 Good Balance Between Opportunity and Risk

    2.9 Regulations and Laws for Cryptocurrencies Taiwan 2018

    2.10 ICOs Self-regulation

    2.11 AML (Anti-money Laundering)

    2.12 Crypto's Legal Classification

    2.13 Taiwan Based Crypto Exchanges

    2.14 Famous Cryptocurrency Exchanges in Taiwan

Chapter 3: Bitopro

    3.1 Utility of BITO Coin

    3.2 Public Sale of Pandacoin and ALLN by Bitopro

    3.3 Learn about Token Exchange Bitopro

    3.4 Business Plan of Bitopro

    3.5 Bitpro- TTCode

       3.5.1 Overview of TT Code

       3.5.2 Usage

       3.5.3 Transaction

       3.5.4 Currency

       3.5.5 Debit Card

       3.5.6 Subscription

       3.5.7 Token Sale

Chapter 4: Max

    4.1 Trading Guidelines for MAX

Chapter 5: Cobinhood

    5.1 Features of Cobinhood

       5.1.1 Trading Fees

       5.1.2 Security System

       5.1.3 Matching Engine of Cobinhood

       5.1.4 High Cloud Performance

       5.1.5 The Application

       5.1.6 Customer Service

       5.1.7 Reserve Guarantee of Cobinhood

       5.1.8 Two-factor Authentication

       5.1.9 Business Model of Cobinhood

       5.1.10 Prime Service

       5.1.11 Trading on High Frequency

       5.1.12 Underwriting Services

       5.1.13 Financial Aspect

    5.2 Dexon and Cobinhood

Chapter 6: JOYSO

    6.1 How does this exchange work?

       6.1.1 Deposit for JOYSO

      6.1.2 Matching on the Platform

      6.1.3 Confirmation on Blockchain

  6.2 Features of JOYSO

  6.3 Difference between Decentralized and Centralized Exchange

      6.3.1 Decentralized Exchange

      6.3.2 Centralized Exchange

      6.3.3 Why is JOYSO called a mixed exchange?

  6.4 Services of JOYSO

      6.4.1 Explaining CEX, DEX and HEX

  6.5 Architecture of JOYSO

  6.6 ICO Market for JOYSO

  6.7 Competition with JOYSO

  6.8 Business Model

  6.9 Marketing Planning

Chapter 7: STAR BIT

  7.1 0x protocol and ZRX

  7.2 Services with Star Bit

  7.3 Decentralized Challenges: EtherDelta, 0x Protocol

  7.4 Principles of Star Bit

  7.5 Star Wallet

  7.6 Token Offerings – Star Bit Token

Chapter 8: Conclusion

Acknowledgement

Chapter 1: Introduction

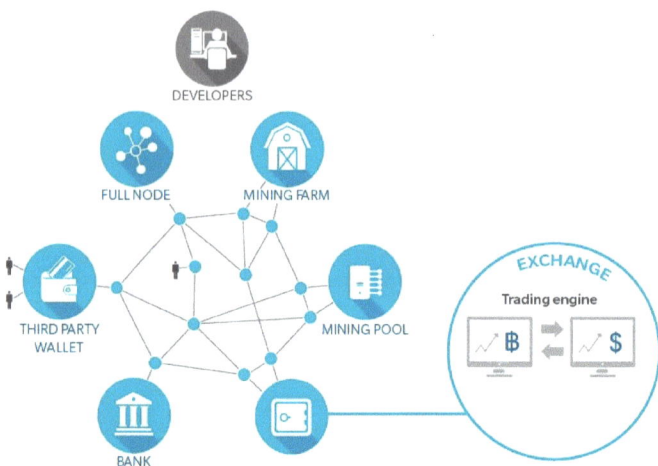

Crypto Exchange, Cryptocurrency Exchange or DCE (digital currency exchange) is a business that allows clienteles to trade digital currencies or cryptocurrencies for other assets or valuables, such as digital currencies or traditional fiat money.

They may act as market maker that are responsible to take each bid and ask spreads as transaction commissions. In this way, they are simply charging a fee for their services as a complementing platform.

Digital currency exchanges can be a brick and mortar business, swapping digital currencies and customary payment method or severely online businesses, switching digital currency and transfer of money electronically.

Several digital currency exchanges are working outside of Western states, avoiding regulatory prosecution and oversight, but DCEs often deal with western fiat currencies or maintain bank accounts in numerous countries to facilitate national currency deposit.

Crypto exchanges may accept wire transfer, credit card payments or payment of other forms in altercation for cryptocurrencies or digital currencies. Regulation of digital exchanges and cryptocurrency is unclear even in several developed jurisdiction. Several regulators are considering the way to deal with these kinds of businesses and regulation commands that are available without any validity test.

These may send digital currencies or cryptocurrency to your cryptocurrency wallet. Several may convert the balances of digital currency into prepaid anonymous cards that are useful for the withdrawal of funds from global ATMs.

Few digital currencies are backed by real-life commodities like gold. Creators of these currencies remain independent of the digital currency exchanges (DCEs) to trade digital currencies. A system urges that DCP (digital currency provider) are businesses that administer and keep accounts for their clients, but don't issue any digital currency directly to their customers.

Customers can sell and buy digital currency form digital currency exchange, who transfer a digital currency out of or into the DCP account of customers. Several DCEs acts as subsidiaries of DCP, but several are lawfully independent businesses. The supremacy of funds available in DCP accounts can be of fictitious or real currencies.

Just like other countries, crypto currency and exchanges are available in Taiwan. Financial supervisory commission of Taiwan has specified its stance on crypto currency remains neutral in spite of current speculation that it was moving toward restrictive policies.

In this paper, we are trying to share facts of crypto exchanges in Taiwan, famous crypto exchanges, digital currencies and regulations to deal with cryptocurrencies in Taiwan. Keep reading to know more about this subject.

Chapter 2: Taiwan Crypto Facts 2018

Contrasting its neighbors, Taiwan is interested to jump on the crypto and blockchain bandwagon. To achieve this goal, it is important to establish particular policies that must support the execution of blockchain technology.

Moreover, Taiwan is focusing in the fine-tuning of its regulatory framework, followed by the certainty that the policies of Taiwan are in accordance with the international standards for the protection of investment. Finally, there must be more discussion to understand the impact of continuation of the development of civic supremacy exploiting technological innovation.

2.1 Blockchain Bandwagon by Taiwan

Chen Mei-ling, theDirector of NDC (National Development Council) of Taiwan had expressed this idea at a Asia Blockchain Summit . Chen said that Taiwan has potential to turn into a hub for cryptocurrencies. It may become a driving force in the 4th revolution of industry that the world is facing this moment.

Once the government of Taiwan chooses to purpose the development of a digital infrastructure, the crypto exchanges may take a leading position in the worldwide economy. NDC is creating in data security office. The office promote digital governance with the use of technologies like blockchain. It may act as an arbitrator between large IT organizations, startup and technology developers in Taiwan.

Taipei Fubon Commercial bank is the first bank of Taiwan to begin a payment system based on blockchain. The bank introduces a system for merchants and restaurants in the nearby vicinity of Federal Chengci University.

The bank is planning to expand this system to businesses and stores across the area of Chengchi area. Taiwan broadcasted that it is not a strict start of different cryptocurrencies like other countries in this region, such as South Korea and China.

Instead, the nation can choose neutral path, following the example of Japan. The government of Taiwan is moving a step further in the development of a legal framework for cryptocurrencies, with the development of Parliamentary Coalition of Taiwan for Blockchain. Led by Jason Hsu Yu-Jen, a legislator, the group intended to bring politician together from different parties. They could create favorable regulations for the development of blockchain and attract investments.

2.2 Asia Blockchain Summit

An important event for the industry of blockchain is organized in Taipei. The Asia Blockchain Summit 2018 is examining the investment opportunities associated with blockchain industry. The Summit analyzes different issues in the development of technology and provides a platform to share ideas on the best regulatory framework in the particular field of cryptocurrencies and blockchain.

2.3 Legitimacy is Increasing the Prices of Digital Currency

Growing legitimacy of digital currencies in Taiwan and other parts of the world is increasing its cost. The currency is frequently getting the major boosts, such as Bitcoin is recognized in Japan as a lawful payment method.

Government validation is not a single point that is increasing the price of Bitcoin. New investments, such as cryptocurrency funds are appeared online. Several startups increase their funding with ICO (initial coin offerings). Instead of trading stock, they are selling bitcoins and bringing millions to their business in investments.

Another reason for the increase in the value of cryptocurrency is hard forks. It may occur when one blockchain splits into two after introduction of new rules and create another cryptocurrency. Past transactions stay on blockchain, but it is not the case with new transactions. Bitcoin cash is a result of hard fork to create billions in the market cap, but lose more than half of its following days. In the future, the investors has to face more hard forks.

2.4 Cryptocurrency Regulations in Taiwan

Taiwan is following moves of its neighbors like South Korea and Japan. Taiwan is planning to roll out new regulations for cryptocurrency on November 2018.

Speaking about anti-money laundering at a conference on April 20, 2018, Justice Minister of Taiwan, Chiu Tai-san said that the Taiwan would develop and implement a specific regulatory framework for digital currencies by this November. The main goal of current regulations may prevent cryptocurrencies from becoming a famous money-laundering instrument.

Government is looking for particular control laws and mechanisms to regulate and govern cryptocurrencies. It will be set by financial services coalition (FSC), ministry of interior and central bank of Taiwan. Legal department of the government ask two crypto exchanges to inform them about different operations in this space.

Chairman FSC Wellington Koo claimed that the present issue with cryptocurrencies is the deficiency of charity surrounding about the purchasers of cryptocurrencies and person selling them again.

They are trying to resolve concerns regarding the market of cryptocurrency and the use of this medium as a money laundering activities. There is an increasing risk of money laundering because of the unregulated nature of cryptocurrency market. The country is hoping to control this threat with the help of certain regulations.

As a part of AML program, the financial service coalition requested banks to list accounts related to crypt-trading platform as "accounts with high risk". It means that if these accounts make a transaction above a particular threshold, banks should notify the regulations who will keep an eye on the activities of these accounts to avoid any potential opportunity of money laundering.

2.5 Taiwan Moves toward Relaxing Cryptocurrency Because of the Constrict Rules in other Countries of Asia

After the arrival of Bitcoin, Taiwan is wondering whether to liberalize or regulate cryptocurrency. The revolutionary digital tokens are supported by transaction ledgers instead of monetary authorities. Important regulations are necessary because these may head off monetary crimes protect established banks concerned about the loss of businesses.

Liberalization is an important step to nurture the domestic monetary technology sector. Signature futuristic hardware of Taiwan gives up the ground of foreign firms. Today, the ruling party and government-dominated legislature show signs of bending toward liberalization. This course is necessary to make it easy to trade Litecoin, Bitcoin and other digital currencies for the better health of fintech sector. The sector is flouring even without strong regulations.

There should be a particular set of frameworks and explanation to position crypto and fundamental technology of blockchain. The position should become a strength for Taiwan, said by Jason Hsu. Jason Hsu is the lawmaker of minority party who is actually pushing regulators and other legislators to favor a playbook on cryptocurrency. There may be a quick switch in the regulations in the future.

2.6 People were Hesitant in the Past

Taiwan has a neutral view on cryptocurrency. Other people in the government re hoping to get more of it. As per Hsu, it is unlawful to solicit cash from the community through tokens of digital currency and efficiently impossible to open a bank account for digital currency.

Several other uses of this currency are not illegal. Two platform based on Taiwan and estimated local 25,000 users trade it. Major banks have their own schemes. Fintech startups include a wallet firm for cryptocurrency and these are popping up in Taiwan. Younger generation is interested to do more with cryptocurrencies.

Officials have their own worries, such as they though that cryptocurrency can allow financial crime, hobble conventional banks of Taiwan and defy taxation. The FSC (Financial Supervisory Commission) notified of "danger" in December just because of the volatility of price in cryptocurrency trading of public.

The ex-chairman of commission Tseng Ming-chung called these currencies illegal in 2015, specifically Bitcoin ATMs. This is his personal opinion. Words of Tseng became the headlines of several newspapers, but he was just sharing his opinions.

2.7 Regulatory Narrowing Overseas

Taiwan may not follow the direction of South Korea and China that banned the fundraisers of cryptocurrency, such as ICOs (initial coin offering).

China is preparing to constrict regulations that can bank cryptocurrency exchanges and ICOs, the newspaper of Taiwan "China Online Daily" claimed in February. Its measurements would enhance monitoring of the accounts of cryptocurrency and step up the supervision of overseas currency flows in ICOs overseas.

South Korea has decided to ban anonymous trading on local exchanges and stopped trades by foreigners. Indian officials are fast-tracking laws for the regulation of trade. On the other hand, Japan overtook China as the major market of Bitcoin around the globe. Almost 58 percent trade of Japan comes from international volume.

Bitcoin is a legal tender in Japan to become crypto-hub in the world. Singapore allows the use of cryptocurrency, but regulates a platform to stop all financial crimes.

2.8 Good Balance Between Opportunity and Risk

Taiwan is trying to seek a balance between innovation of cryptocurrency and protection of consumers from greedy practices. People want to see the execution of new technology for their protection.

Volatility for digital currencies is an important concern for a long duration and governments are worried about the pump-and-dump tactics that they are seeing. Officials of Taiwan have drafted a version of guidelines.

2.9 Regulations and Laws for Cryptocurrencies Taiwan 2018

Taiwan is making progress toward establishing itself as a hub for ICOs (initial coin offerings) and businesses based on blockchain. There are not particular regulations and laws for cryptocurrencies. The government of Taiwan has a positive attitude toward this blossoming industry and ambitions to develop specific rules for anti-money laundering to cryptocurrencies by November of this year.

The government of Taiwan is discussing the development of further regulations for ICOs. It is a hope for the proponents of the industry that the necessity for government oversight may be decreased through the self-regulation of the industry.

It is predictable that the development in countries like Switzerland, the US and other states with mature laws may be heavily referred to the government of Taiwan and self-regulating organizations in the development of specific rules of Taiwan for cryptocurrency and requirements of self-regulation model.

2.10 ICOs Self-regulation

Jason Hsu – legislator of Taiwan – explained in an article of 2017 that position of Taiwan on ICOs is designed as three no-polices. The government of Taiwan doesn't encourage, prohibit or take accountability for it.

This method is viewed as a significant chance for ICOs to terrestrial in Taiwan. In order to allow the government of Taiwan to maintain a hands-off position, a growing number of researchers, scholars, ventures and proponents of ICOs promoter for the self-regulated ICOs as a mechanism to protect the rights of investors.

As per this background, 22 May is an important day known as a Pizza Day in the community of blockchain. This day is important for two initiatives that were introduced to facilitate Taiwan becoming a special crypto island. These are TBSRO (Taiwan Crypto Blockchain Self-Regulatory Organization) and TPCB (Taiwan Parliamentary Coalition for Blockchain).

The TPCB refers to a cross-party association with the goal of deciding and developing on a flawless regulatory structure for the segment of blockchain through building trust and education between the players of cryptocurrency industry and regulators.

The TBSRO intends to decrease the need of extra oversight of government and allow government to take supportive approach towards the industry of blockchain by demanding its members to conform to transparency and mechanisms of investor protection.

Fintech Taiwan Association (FTA) is co-founded by Tsai Jaclyn (he is a founding person of Lee Tsai and Partners). This organization will lead TBSRO. Under the leader of Tsai, the FTA is establishing a global IC transparency platform with worldwide leaders in the industry of ICO to bridge the information gap between investors and issuers of ICO.

With powerful self-regulatory tools for the protection of investors, the necessity for the regulations of government may be decreased.

2.11 AML (Anti-money Laundering)

Because of anonymous and decentralized nature of digital currencies, the government of Taiwan is worried with the prospective that they can be used for crime and illegal transactions. Taiwan is a member of Asia-Pacific group on the subject of money laundering. Taiwan follows the recommendations of the financial task action force that is responsible to set global policies for anti-money laundering.

Obligations include a specific risk-based approach, CDD (customer due diligence, licensing and registration requirements, mitigation and identification of associated risks with latest technologies, record-keeping, reporting of suspicious transaction and requirements for AML program.

Almost 35 countries and a European commission is asked FATF to improve the requirement of AML for cryptocurrency. The FATF is reviewing different standards related to cryptocurrencies. FATF may adopt latest standards similar to those currencies implemented in South Korea: banning unidentified trading of cryptocurrencies, the outline of real-name system and severe regulations on the verifications of client's identities.

On May 2018, the Justice Ministry, the Financial Supervisory Commission of Taiwan (FSC), the CBT (Central Bank of Taiwan) and the Bureau of Economic Dealings jointly stated that several industries related to Bitcoin have to comply with the Money Laundering Act. It is expected that the specific guidelines for AML cryptocurrencies will be finalized by November 2018. It may incorporate the updated guidelines of FATF.

2.12 Crypto's Legal Classification

The CBT and FSC announced that digital currencies are classified as commodities instead of a currency. The position of FSC for other cryptocurrencies is related to the securities subject to SEA (security exchange act) of Taiwan.

As per 6th articles of the SEA, these securities are defined as corporate bonds, corporate stocks and government bonds and other securities are approved by competent authority, such as the FSC.

The Finance Ministry of Taiwan clarified that beneficiary certificates, government bonds, corporate bonds, foreign stocks and several other securities with the particular investment nature are offered, traded and issued in Taiwan. These must be subject to SEA.

Similar to several jurisdictions, the prerogative of the issuer is linked to the fortitude that an instrument is a security token traded, offered or issued in Taiwan or a security may be subject to the security exchange act (SEA).

Taiwan will follow the approach of the Securities and Exchange Commission and determine the legal status and classification of virtual tokens as per each case. There will be no court cases in Taiwan particularly determining whether these tokens are securities. The High Court in Taiwan in 2011 adopted a particular Howey test. This test is designed by the supreme court of the US in the 1946 to determine whether contracts related to foreign investment are securities.

After evaluation of Howey test, there are four important considerations:

- Is it an important investment in money?
- Is there a revenue sharing from an investment?
- Is it a mutual enterprise?
- Does the revenue come from the hard work of others?

The high court of Taiwan determines that interests in foreign companies with limited liability are securities. Finally, the sale of interest is subject to SEA and it is regulated by FSC.

Howey test is applied by the District Court in Taiwan during a case of 2014 that limited interest in partnerships also establish securities. Considering this trend in the courts of Taiwan, you can expect that this test can be similarly used to determine whether the virtual tokes are securities. These securities will be regulated by the oversight of FSC and the SEA.

Currently, the chairperson of FSC , Wellington Koo, specified that tokens of ICO must be classified into three important categories: payment type, security type and utility type tokens. It is similar to an approach of Financial Market Swiss Supervisor Authority (FINMA) that created these categories as per the specification of tokens:

- **Payment Tokens:** These tokens can be used to make payment for acquiring services and goods or as a source of value or money transfer.
- **Asset Tokens:** These are virtual tokens to represent one asset, such as equity of issuer and a claim of debt.
- **Utility Tokens:** These virtual tokens can provide digital access to a service or application with the use of an infrastructure based on blockchain.

The FSC may put a robust consideration on the guidelines of FINMA in determining its particular future approach regarding classification of token. Moreover, based on trends from past, several financial regulations of Taiwan are developed from the regulations of SEC (security exchange commission). The attitude of SEC toward digital or cryptocurrency can affect the view of Taiwan government for ICOs.

Just like other jurisdictions, if tokens are classified as security, the issuance and offering of the token may be subject to SEA regulations for public offers in Taiwan, unless it qualifies exemption from private placement.

You can expect a major development in Taiwan in the coming months for the rules of cryptocurrencies. Cryptocurrency issuers and blockchain businesses are taking decision on their jurisdiction. They want a close monitoring of these developments. These steps may help Taiwan to become suitable jurisdiction for the incorporation of cryptocurrencies.

2.13 Taiwan Based Crypto Exchanges

Crypto Exchanges are sites where you can trade cryptocurrencies for traditional currencies like Euro or US dollars or digital currencies. These exchanges offers services to sell, buy or exchange digital assets and cryptocurrency to other digital assets or fiat currency.

These businesses allow customers to trade their digital currencies for other assets like traditional fiat money or digital currencies. They may act as market makers that take the ask/bid spreads as a specific commission of transaction for their services or charge fees as matching platforms.

Exchanges of digital currency can be brick-and-mortar businesses, digital currencies, and exchanging customary payment methods or swapping electronically transferred money, strict online business and famous digital currencies.

The higher volume of trading on an available crypto-exchange proves that the users are trusting on these exchanges. Higher trading volume means capital outflow and inflow from the market. A huge trading volume on the given market is a display of the sentimentality about traded assets.

If the rate is increasing with increase in volumes, it shows that capital inflows to crypto market. Similarly, huge fall in rates together with the trading volumes displays that the cash is flying from the marketplace.

Experienced dealers from other markets like Forex or Stock markets, are ready to trade professionally on a crypto exchange with high liquidity, trading with excellent volume, getting the trading volume of exchanges may be time-consuming and tasking.

The coinmarketcap offers the updated and accurate data on crypto-exchanges and cryptocurrencies. It will be good to spend your time to make verifications on the collection of data from different exchanges. You have to make sure to check your trading volume on differences sources instead of relying on data provided by an exchange.

2.14 Famous Cryptocurrency Exchanges in Taiwan

To decrease your stress of selecting the right exchange in Taiwan, we have a comprehensive list containing the famous exchanges.

As mentioned, people earn through cryptocurrencies in many parts of the world including Taiwan. Here the crypto exchanges from Taiwan are being introduced briefly with understanding the main exchanges of crypto like Bitopro, Max, Cobinhood, JOYSO and Star Bit. The operational usage of these exchanges will be explained as well as their unique features out of which you can bring benefit to your accounts.

Chapter 3: Bitopro

BitoPro is a crypto exchange developed by the team of BitoEX. It is started to provide a reliable solution of cryptocurrency, such as financial auditing, business application, digital wallet and more.

Team of BitoEX is committed to lead an industry of digital currency. This exchange offers comprehensive services to customers in unique branding and excellent quality. BitoEX is expected to offer an easy procedure to enter the digital currency for everyone.

Highlights

- It is the best wallet serve in Taiwan.
- The 5th in the volume around the world.
- More than 3000 suitability stores in Taiwan.
- Top ten APEC Payment Solution 2017 Companies
- Over 200,000 Unique members

BitoPro International Exchange for Digital Assets target global investors. It is successfully operating trading services and Bitcoin wallets in Taiwan. BtioPro facilitates users with management function, important tools for risk management, management of advanced assets, customer support on platform and ability to meet the needs of customers.

Business scope of BitoPro includes relevant derivatives and cryptocurrency trading services like leverage trading, crypto-financing, crypto-to-crypto trading and fiat trading. BitPro is planning to provide an inclusive solution to the problem by offering worldwide investors the capability to utilize TT code to withdraw and deposit local fiat currencies at this platform.

On this platform, users will need BITO Coin that is a token issued through BitoPro Digial asset exchange. You can get favorable discounts by using coins as a withdraw fee or source of transaction.

3.1 Utility of BITO Coin

BITO Coin Use	BITO Coin Description	Mode of Use
Transaction Fee	Transaction fee approximately 0.1% - 0.2%	Discount
Withdrawal Fee	Withdrawal fees may be adjusted based on the actual circumstances of the blockchain.	Discount
Financing Transaction	Participation in loan provision services to collect loan interest and pay loan provision fees	Discount
Local Fiat Currency Withdrawal	Generation of TT Code for the withdrawal of legal tender	Limited to BITO Coins
BitoPro Debit Card	Purchasing or topping up BitoPro Debit Cards	Limited to BITO Coins
Token Marketing	Token launch marketing service fees	Limited to BITO Coins
Token Subsctiption	Advance participation in supplied tokens	Limited to BITO Coins
Token Sales on BitoPro	Trading fees for promising tokens	Limited to BITO Coins
Token Airdrop	Based on user-held BITO Coin proportions, provide airdrop tokens	Limited to BITO Coins

Sales volume of BITO Coin is anticipated to over 500 million tokens and this number is subject to change. The ratio of toke allocation is expected to almost 35 percent with an extra reserve of 25 percent for subscription.

Bitopro is known as the project which issues the tokens related to cryptocurrency. It is one form of digital currency used while getting into the world of cryptocurrency. It is an ICO which is provided by the investors to have the tokens to get exchanged while working with the digital currencies. This is one of those type of tokens which are limited according to time and the funds which are raised. The goods which get traded in cryptocurrency help in building up embodies in cryptocurrency.

Some of the examples may include points, coins, game items and more. The tokens of Bitopro can certainly be used as the company's share to be presented as the cryptocurrency. In the near future, the trend of Bitpro may be rising and reach as to become the biggest company in trading. The traders working with Bitpro are professional and certified to work with cryptocurrency. The achievements within the company has acquired numerous assets to begin and lead in the market. Bitpro got introduced in the market in 2016 end.

The technology of blockchain helps efficiently in SCM (Supply Chain Management). It helps in tracing and making the things cost-effective in the nature of SCM. The movement of the material, tracing, acquiring information, recording and more can be done easily on blockchain. The processes are defined clearly with making sure that everything is getting done on time along with being visible to all the relative parties involved.

You are able to reach back at point one through blockchain technology when it is about SCM. It makes the processes feasible for the businesses to locate their goods and the entire process. The investigations on the process can be done easily through blockchain. It helps in making the right execution of actions when needed to maintain high quality of material. A good example can be of the perishable items to maintain their quality throughout until it reaches the end customer.

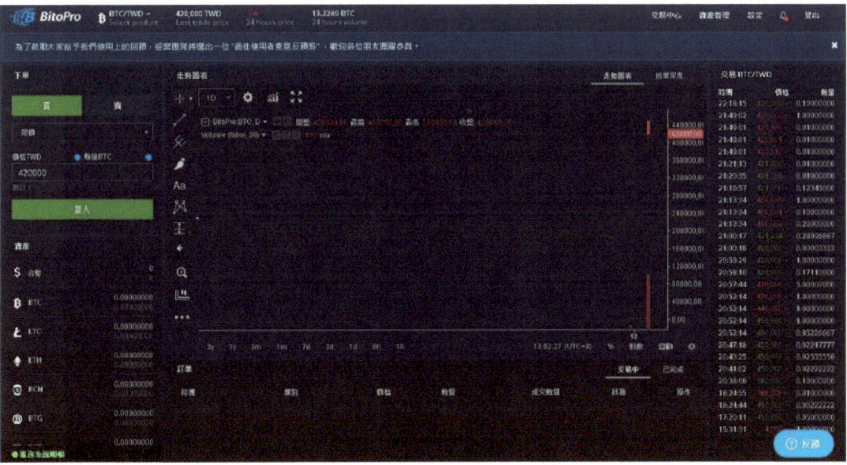

The transactions get recorded on Bitopro and with that, there is less change of error in the system and information entered. The data is protected and no one is able to change it. The verification of records is done when the information passes through one user to another as it is a peer-to-peer connection. It keeps the record accurate without any discrepancy.

You are able to work efficiently in terms of accounting with organized manner. Without having many ledgers at the same time, everything will be available for the business owners to view on the blockchain network. All the records can be found under one network easily with keeping a consistent track as well. It remains secured and no one is able to misuse the information under any circumstances.

Businesses can have a bad impact when transactions take time. The process of communication needs to be quick and should be consistent. You can find that easily on blockchain. Having the compatibility with smart contracts through Bitopro can help you acquire business information within few minutes. You can easily get the automatic validation over blockchain. There is no need for any medium source which is why companies prefer it nowadays because it saves their time. Businesses can work through the services integration without disclosing much of their information to the other party.

The elections on governance are made easier through blockchain where there is no chance of manipulation. As it is impossible to change the information, the true voting results can come out through blockchain network. It helps in getting the right person for the government which can eliminate the electoral fraud on their end. With the concept of easy voting, there are many companies who adopted the e-voting systems to find proper solutions of transparency in their systems.

Trading has been common on blockchain technology. It is no surprise that blockchain would surely support stock exchange. The stock exchange of Australia is already on the verge to get started with system of blockchain powered. They are going to invest in the distributed ledger according to their records found in December 2017.

Businesses either worry about the bills which they receive or do not care where the expenses of energy come from. The blockchain transactive grids help to conserve the energy at many parts of the world. It works as a great energy solution for many commercial companies out there. It keeps the energy clean and tracked easily as well.

If you have understood the basics of blockchain, then you would surely know what peer to peer transactions are. It helps businesses to work through blockchain in order to exchange the currencies through cryptocurrencies especially when it is about international payment transfers. They are secure to handle along with having the freedom with the transfer of their own funds. It is not long that almost all the business owners will start following the distributed ledgers. For

Some a distributed channel is a concern but they are observing the trend of it and as it rises, they would be joining the network soon too.

With having a rapid base of clients on blockchain, the innovation over the network increases. The communities which get build through the blockchain technology has some of the limitations which come along. Some of the flaws which get overlooked by the clients but still exist. There are some of the issues which were addresses by the experts when they looked closely into the blockchain technology and its functions.

It started with the selling and purchase of bitcoins by the traders with building up through the investors. The participation of investors and traders combined led the company to grow over the period of time. Everyone working with Bitpro tends to have the same base and faith for the cryptocurrency which keeps the unity among all the participants. The volatility of bitcoin is above all other currencies which makes it a propounding one in the world of cryptocurrency.

3.2 Public Sale of Pandacoin and ALLN by Bitopro

There are fair examples of Pandacoin team which leads to the terms of integrity. Without having any ICO behind, the work over the team is with fair terms and honesty. The team does not prefer to have any discussions over the costs with having no policy initially. Pandacoin makes it easier for people to understand the world of cryptocurrency. The investors who are eager to learn can surely participate in Pandacoin to learn about the main features.

https://www.bitopro.com/token_exchange/index

3.3 Learn about Token Exchange Bitopro

The currency exchange of Bitopro is available online in the form of cryptocurrency. The platform offers users to have exchange of tokens to have their own robots to trade. It helps in making the charts and learn the flow of the market. The users of cryptocurrency are able to trade the tokens in the market to have real time earning.

The team of BitoEX created the Bitopro exchange tokens. It was issued in 2014 to give the opportunity to the user in trading these cryptocurrencies. The solution provided were the applications, wallets and auditing the transactions online.

The team is based in Taiwan with having the contacts internationally. There are more than 2000 stores in Taiwan having members up to 300,000 in this platform. The API of the company can provide you the Bitopro exchange tokens or you can create by yourself.

The decision of using the tokens then you will most likely receive the trading services on the standard basis. There is fee attached to each trade and if you are wanting the trading of coins then you can sell them when the trend is high and make the purchase when they are low at price. The trends keep on fluctuating so you have to keep a keen eye on it.

You can keep the track of the exchange tokens by Bitopro with having full advantage of the platform. The wallet has all your records which you can refer to whenever you want to do it. The smartphone application is available for the users to download to have the instant access. You are able to keep track over the transactions anywhere without being restricted to the laptops/computers. You can trade the tokens with any person on the platform through this software. You do not need to provide all the information to have the access to the account which is why it is convenient and easy to set up on your smartphones.

3.4 Business Plan of Bitopro

To be successful in the competitive market, there are business plans which are setup from the companies to proceed further. The step by step process helps in achieving the goals which are determined by the company. It helps the company to reach its goal by being consistent on the goal with keeping the check over it. Here are some of the steps which are mentioned in the plan of Bitopro and can help you reach where you aim to as well.

- It starts with the registration of client with Bitopro. The deposit of BPC is required to get started. The deposit BPC can be done through ethereum or bitcoin. It needs to be deposited in the wallet of the company with making the conversion into BPC.
- The payout for the deposited amount will be by 30% through the capital investment. The addition of payouts are done on the wallet starting the next day. The result of

participation is done on daily basis. The rewards are provided to the clients within 6 month time as they start after the deposit.

- The profit over the account can be withdrawal whenever the client wants. The conversion done by the client is logged in with having the balance of minimal BPC 2000 in the account.
- The last step for this plan is over the investment. Any or new members are able to participate in the investments. They have to acquire the code of referral with having the profit of 5%. The decision of withdrawal is only the decisions of the member who earns the money. The profit is earned over the BPC is through the price which is in trend on the cryptocurrency. There are multiple accounts which are held accountable when you have big investments on the account. Earning daily profits is a big part of it which is why it is one of the famous company for trading.

3.5 Bitpro- TTCode

3.5.1 Overview of TT Code

TT Code is the type of token which is used in the Bitpro blockchain platform as the digital asst. the transactions and the withdrawals are free of cost with keeping the discounts under consideration with this amazing TT Code.

The permitted laws within Bitpro works as the generation of TT Code which is denominated as the local currency in the legal terms. The operations are held within the payment of the coins and the sales of tokens which get accessed by TT Code and some may require the issuance fee along with it when you have to make the payment of the sales.

The functions of Bitpro are able to provide discounts which are there for the fees and transactional access to the accounts. When you have the costs included, you can keep the fees with currencies which are digitally available and working over the fees of transactions. The balances are sufficient to keep the cause of producing coins with the calculated balances which are involved in the currencies. The fees of transactions are able to produce marketing tokens which prove to be beneficial for the users only.

According to the expansion of market, the rate of TT Code may fluctuate with keeping the services fee in control. The subscription can be accessed with its launch and you can have the advance payments within control of keeping the rights of coins offered in the cryptocurrencies. So basically, you will be receiving the discounts at the same time of accessing the TT Code.

3.5.2 Usage

The application of Bitpro TT Code uses certain jurisdictions which are there to imply on the functions. The introductions of the laws are there for the discounts which get offered to the clients.

Having the fees which are favorable for the clients or sometimes, there are discounts which can be offered on the basis of usage of the account. The value of the account increases as the time passes with knowing that the interest is there for the provisions of loans which you can enjoy over the period of time.

The platform allows you to keep the payments within the interest of services which you can keep the transactions smooth and operational every time.

3.5.3 Transaction

The transactions of TT Code is done through the Bitpro coin with keeping the lower costs of it. Within the transactions, there are digital currencies involved which helps you in generating the coins automatically to keep the rise of balance consistent in your account once you are a regular user of Bitpro.

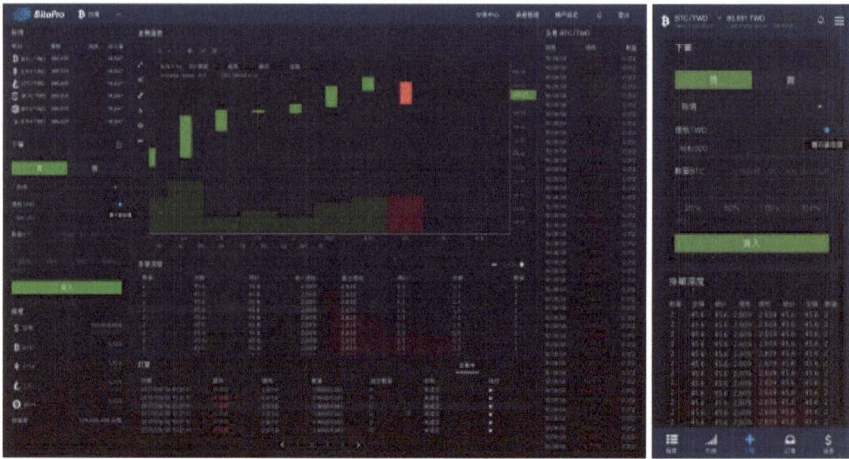

The balances keep on rising with getting the right value of coin calculate through the system upon usage. You also get to receive the discounts through transitions with the passage of time.

3.5.4 Currency

The transactions get done in the form of digital currency which gets deposited in your account with having the services financially. Entire plan is defined for the payments and the transactions which you can use as a loan or for your cash payments in the future. The services will require to keep the incur fee on the services with having many platforms on the discounts or fees associated with it.

There can be fees for the payments depending upon the amount which gets coursed by you as the time passes within the course of action with TT Code.

3.5.5 Debit Card

When it is about the debit card with TT Code, you have the right to withdraw money through it. You will have to purchase the Bitpro debit card which you can use to withdraw the currencies locally from any bank. The ATMs will be operational for this debit card when it is valid and for the transactions if you wish to make any from it when you go out for shopping or when you wish to shop online as well.

The costs of the top ups will be updated in the system of Bitpro which can add up the coins for TT Code in your account.

3.5.6 Subscription

The launch of the token is done through subscription which is available at the Bitpro section of TT Code. The offerings are done by the cryptocurrencies which are offered through the discounts.

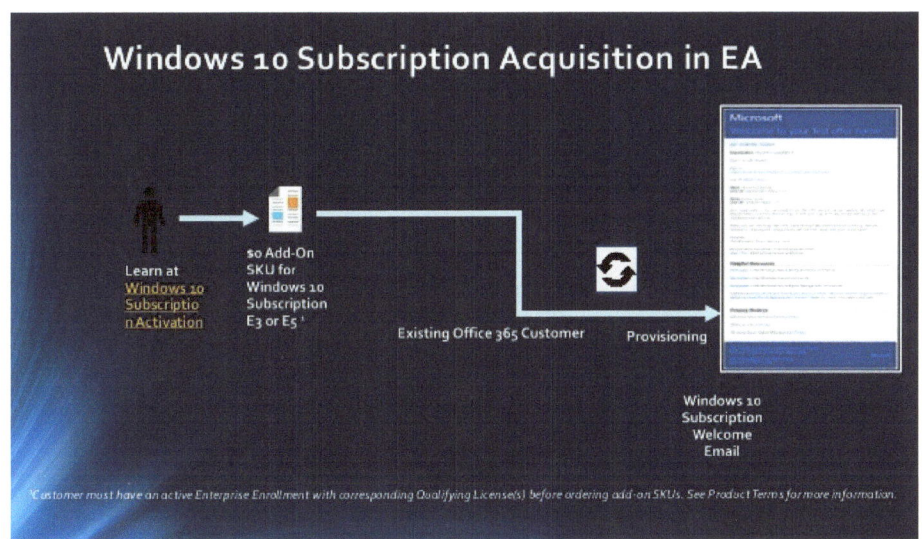

When the token sales get provided on the basis of centers which are operational, they can be supplied to the matter of providing detailed version which is available on the course. You have to keep the discounts applied within the matter of time as they launch in the public domain.

The supplies are already prepared for the subscriptions for the users so you just have to make the purchase through the token sales.

3.5.7 Token Sale

The sale of tokens get planned by the Bitpro and TT Code within the supply of cryptocurrencies. The centers are able to operate within the anticipation of keeping the launch of promising situations which are therefore the right of keeping within the fees of coins. The promising cryptocurrencies working with collecting the right fee of token sales with providing discounts to the users at the same time.

Chapter 4: Max

MaiCoin is the largest digital asset platform of Taiwan. The similar team has not developed a new exchange for digital assets known as MAX to serve community in a better way. Users are allowed to trade digital assets, such as Litecoin, Ethereum, and Bitcoin with the use of NTD among all participants of the market.

Taiwan Dollar is an amazing feature of this exchange. The assets of NTD (Taiwan dollar) are safely stored in the custody of 3rd party, KGI Investment Trust. Their team has top technologists, customer service personnel and security engineer. Your security is their priority so they offer reliable digital financial peer-to-peer service to their customers.

They are working to empower the self-sovereign persons through distributed unanimity technology. They want to offer a top-rated, secure, low cost and fast digital exchange where people can trade directly.

Order Book						Market Trades		
Total	Volume	BID	ASK	Volume	Total	Time	Price	Volume
16,979.9	1.216332	13,960.0	14,177.3	1.000000	14,177.3	15:07:26	14,000.0 ▼	0.055165
40,350.0	2.892480	13,950.0	14,188.0	1.000000	14,188.0	15:07:25	14,000.0 ▼	0.010735
1,394.9	0.100000	13,949.0	14,196.0	4.500000	63,882.0	15:07:25	14,001.0 ▼	0.414100
13,947.0	1.000000	13,947.0	14,197.0	1.500000	21,295.5	15:01:35	14,109.0 ▲	0.138882
13,902.0	1.000000	13,902.0	14,199.0	1.000000	14,199.0	14:55:43	14,109.0 ▲	0.275195
20,851.5	1.500000	13,901.0	14,200.0	1.923356	27,311.6	14:55:43	14,000.0 ▲	0.079805
176,916.3	12.727792	13,900.0	14,227.0	0.732318	10,418.6	14:48:58	14,000.0 ▼	0.000195
13,880.0	1.000000	13,880.0	14,247.0	1.495345	21,304.1	14:47:07	14,000.0 ▼	0.285519
6,233.4	0.450000	13,852.0	14,250.0	1.000000	14,250.0	14:47:07	14,000.0 ▼	0.004481
						14:41:25	14,000.0 ▼	0.600000
						14:37:53	14,000.0 ▼	0.374090
						14:37:53	14,000.0 ▼	0.982150

In MAX, community and users can get maximum facilities. They want to empower the concept that the internet is connecting the whole world and economy. The future of an economy lies in open financial systems. With the use of digital currency, the world can be a better place with equal opportunities and freedom.

4.1 Trading Guidelines for MAX

If you want to trade, you must have enough balance of Fiat currency or digital currency to convert the value of order and applicable fees. A valid order will be instantly placed on the appropriate Order Book. It will become eligible to match to conforming. Orders placed by MAX users at a suitable price and on the first time will get priority. A trader has to follow a Stop Order, Market Order or Limit Order. A dealer can cancel orders with open limits without any time restriction before filing it. You can cancel any order without worrying about a fee. An order will be Taker or Maker Orders. A taker order can immediately match with the current order on an order book. A Maker order may not get immediate matching with one order on an order book and subsequently becomes a part of order book. Charges may vary for Taker and Maker Order.

Limit Orders

It is an order to sell or buy a particular quantity of assets at a particular price. This order will be filled at an improved or specified price. There is no guarantee to fill this order because of large fluctuation and low liquidity on an order book. This order can be a Taker Order or a Maker Order. It the limit of an order is complimenting the current Maker Order, the order can be a Taker Order.

Market Orders

It is an order to purchase and sell immediately particular quality of assets at the best available rate on an order book. There is no guarantee that an order will be filled at a specific price. The order may be filled at different prices as per the quantity of market orders and current orders on an Order Book at a particular time.

Based on the prices and volume of orders on an order book, the market order may be filled at a less favorable price than current trade prices. It is known as a slippage. This is an overview. Other order are also available so you must consider their site to learn more about orders.

Limit of Orders

See the chart of regular limits. These limits are subject to change and the deposit amounts of NTD may surpass the limits. These excessive amounts can be returned to a verified bank account.

Transaction limits	Deposit	Withdrawal Limit
New Taiwan Dollar (NTD) Daily	$2,000,000 NTD	$2,000,000 NTD
New Taiwan Dollar (NTD) Monthly	$10,000,000 NTD	$10,000,000 NTD
BTC Bitcoin (Daily)	Unlimited	$160,000 USD
ETH Ethereum (Daily)	Unlimited	$160,000 USD
LTC Litecoin (Daily)	Unlimited	$160,000 USD
MITH Mithril (Daily)	Unlimited	$160,000 USD
BCH Bitcoin Cash (Daily)	Unlimited	$160,000 USD
USDT (Daily)	Unlimited	$160,000 USD
TRX (Daily)	Unlimited	$160,000 USD
CCCX (Daily)	Unlimited	$160,000 USD
PAL (Daily)	Unlimited	$160,000 USD

Market	Minimum Order Size	Minimum Order Volume
BTC/TWD	$10 NTD	0.00000001 BTC
ETH/TWD	$10 NTD	0.000001 ETH
LTC/TWD	$10 NTD	0.0001 LTC
MITH/TWD	$10 NTD	0.01 MITH
BCH/TWD	$10 NTD	0.000001 BCH
USDT/TWD	$10 NTD	0.01 USDT
TRX/TWD	$10 NTD	0.1 TRX
CCCX/TWD	$10 NTD	0.1 CCCX
PAL/TWD	$10 NTD	0.1 PAL

Chapter 5: Cobinhood

The currency of Cobinhood is for the upcoming generation on the platform of cryptocurrency. The future of the economy is based over the financials and in the era of blockchain, there are more certainty over the economy as the earning is high for most of the people out there. People who dream about earning a lot of money can take advantage of Cobinhood to earn money online through digital currency.

There is no trading fee involved when you are working with the Cobinhood whether you are trading bitcoin, ethereum or any other digital currency. The traders wish to have the ultimate maximization to earn profits on the edge. The assets are deposited in the Cobinhood which is opened only on the basis of security.

COBINHOOD stores the majority of crypto assets deposited in multisig offline vault that needs 5 out of 8 hardware geo-distributed security components to open. Moreover, crypto assets stowed in reliable online wallets. The wallets keep the security with having online reliable sources which are backed by the insurance online. There are multiple orders which get processed on Cobinhood on daily basis. The distribution process of Cobinhood is popular which makes a great experience for traders over the platform. Traders are able to make complete use of it with earning high profits through this platform.

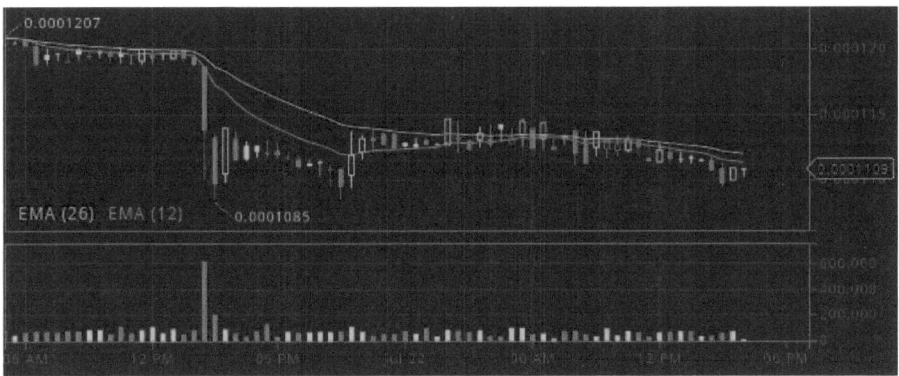

COBINHOOD's patented order corresponding engine may process millions of online orders with sub-millisecond latency. The entire system is designed to distributed completely and highly available as well as auto scalable to achieve an ultimate trading experience. This platform will give an ultimate trading experience to all traders around the world.

The cryptocurrency of Cobinhood may seem to have risk with the larger requirements over the period of time. There are some propositions attached to it which can compare the market and the picking of the truth. You are able to increase the volume with the trading and the stocks with it. The financial situation helps in keeping the existence of the bitcoin before the year of 2009. There are many opportunities which are attached to Cobinhood and you are able to become a great trader out of it.

5.1 Features of Cobinhood

There are multiple features associated with Cobinhood which you have to learn before you get started with the cryptocurrency and its associates.

5.1.1 Trading Fees

With having the fee of trading under consideration, there are leverages which have to be followed under the maximum profit around the world. With the guaranteed of the reserves, the disclosures are made with the wallet which are present there along with the audit options. You have to keep the funds with the trading making it public without any ensuring policy of trying to disclose over the estimated cost of trading and its funds published. Having the assets which get deposited over time should be able to get the offline storage and the wallet will have increase of up to 97% assets.

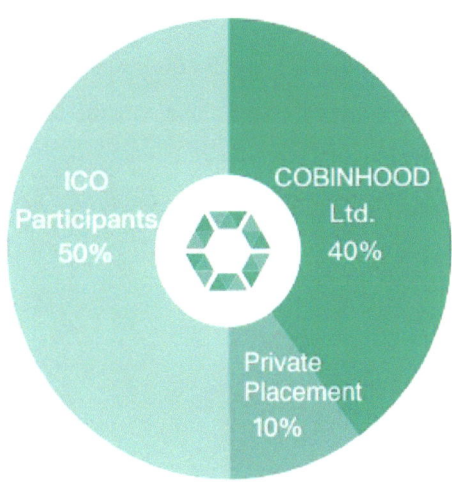

5.1.2 Security System

The security system of the wallets have clear transactions which are available for the audits publicly. You can aim for the profits more than 90% of the times with keeping the funds on the trading option for offline stores. The online transactions allow you to keep the wallet in a faster usage to enhance the overall experience as well. The HSMs will be produced up to 5 out of 9 options which makes it feasible over the period of time. If there is not any distribution within the platform then you have to keep the assets with its coverage. Along with the deposits, there are enforcements which are followed by Cobinhood which work with the authentication processes along with confirmation of the product online. The speed comes exceptional knowing that the engines need to be matched over the period of time. The composition of the micro services which are included at the backend of the Cobinhood need to have the que and the matching services which you can keep under consideration.

5.1.3 Matching Engine of Cobinhood

Another interesting feature would be the design and the matching policy of Cobinhood with the assets which you are trying to purchase online. With having the right order and the speed of matching, you can easily keep the orders within the specific type of information which you require for pairing the transmitted information through the system.

Keeping the engine matching for the sources can be combine with the Docker and the spanner which is available on the high resolution for the scales. Knowing the records can keep the scaling which is there for the auto processing along with the consistency which you can aim for keeping the scales in order.

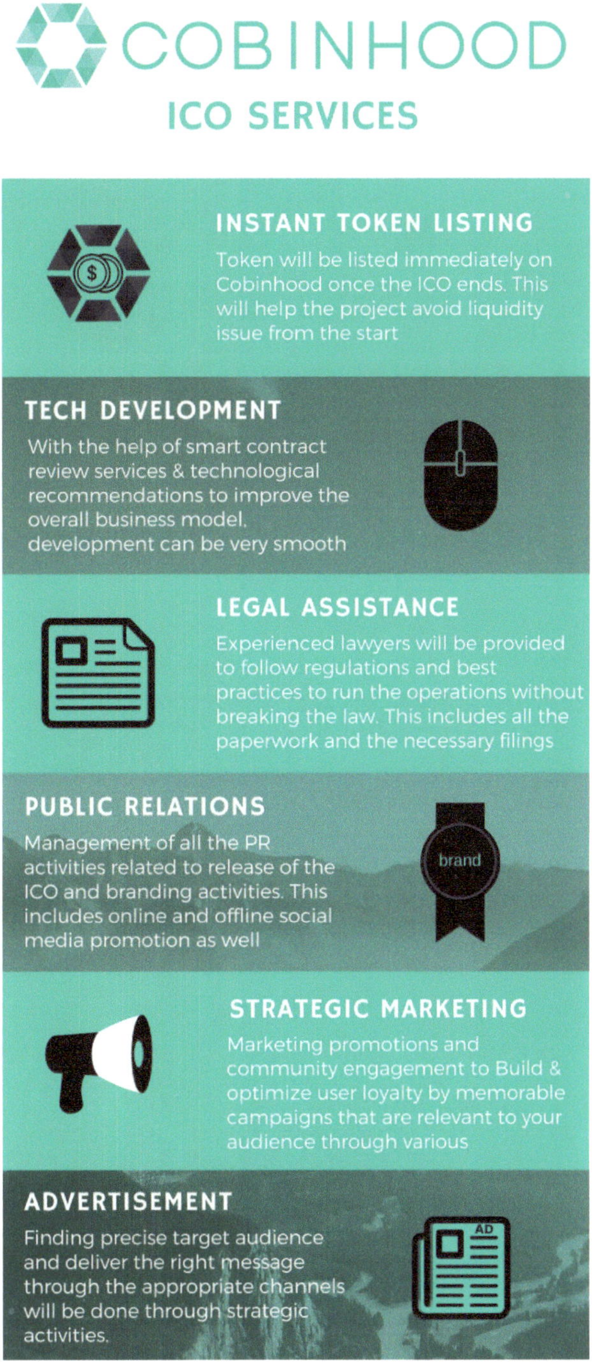

5.1.4 High Cloud Performance

The transactions keep the record of keeping the consistent and available cluster which is there to keep the memory on the technology up to the replication of memory. The transactions need to have the updated which are sent by the protocol of WAMP to the system for easy access of information. The information is available for the real time experience with keeping the drive development of the features along with keeping the strength of the system with the integration strong as well. The capability of performance seems to be high with Cobinhood comparatively to other cryptocurrencies. With keeping the ranges flat and able to have the exchanges in the services, there are some of the languages which you can create to keep it supportive for yourself.

5.1.5 The Application

The application of Cobinhood proves to be among the right coverage of cryptocurrencies within the supportive system. Having the right support of languages work well within the transactions and their processing is faster too. There are different languages which Cobinhood supports such as Russian, English, French, Japanese and more.

5.1.6 Customer Service

The customer service is always available to help you sort out any issues which you may be facing with the system. The representatives actively help out the users to make sure that they are able to run it smoothly on their systems. The help can be achieved for the system or the application of the Cobinhood if there is any trouble which you are not able to sort out. All the help is available every time you contact them so you do not have to be time bound.

With having certain goal in the mind, there are some of the processes which you have to be consistent and being able to provide consistent customer service is one of the main features of Cobinhood. The identification services of Cobinhood provide the services without any time limit so you can access the system through a proper gate and channel easily.

The team of Cobinhood provides assistance of various projects of Cobinhood which can be there for the consensus along with keeping the feasibility on the board. The frequency can be high with measuring over the time and real time experiences with the clients along with investors. Keeping the ICO projects on the goal, you have to measure over the contracts which are smart to handle and keep them underwritten as well.

The team will be able to review the projects with keeping Cobinhood aligned with the tokens which are of high quality. They can be traded along with the ICO and be the launch on the enterprises system knowing the reviews on legal systems. You will be get through the enterprises which are known to the systems to keep the diligence pass through the compliances legally.

5.1.7 Reserve Guarantee of Cobinhood

Keeping the reserve and guarantee of Cobinhood under consideration, it is 100% secured. The online transactions and wallets are held with no unknown failures. The funds get transferred without any worry of being disclosed to any third party. The information is not even shared with any of the two parties who are indulged in continuing their transactions online.

5.1.8 Two-factor Authentication

With having the two factor authentication to sign in, it provides the security to the user of accessing their system by themselves. It ensures that no one else is there to hold the account or transactions with the personal authentication which is not shared with anyone. If there is a withdrawal within the system then an email of confirmation is sent in order to make sure that it is the real person whose account it is to hold the information. You have to keep the system secured on your end in order to keep the assets and cryptocurrencies safe.

The documentations need to be there with keeping the technology of blockchain consistent and keeping the traditional accounts. The program will be able to examine the compliance with the help of players within the smart contracts. The technology keeps on launching with having the individuals keep their own ICO and fundraising for their accomplishment throughout. The enterprises will be able to measure through the guidance and there will be people who will notably find the image of mining online easily. Keeping it fairly simple to launch, the features provide you ease of working out with Cobinhood and their ICOs to manage it conveniently online.

5.1.9 Business Model of Cobinhood

There are total of four points which you have to follow when you are working on the business model of Cobinhood. The users are able to identify it easily with keeping the trading margin under consideration. The deposits can be made with the rate of interest knowing the demand and their supply. Keeping the earnings within the demand, Cobinhood has the ability to keep the capabilities and assets collected throughout.

5.1.10 Prime Service

Along with the consistent review of services, there are traders which measure upon the leverages and their trading is slower than before. You have to keep the limits and rates within the exchanges of Cobinhood so it can be measured easily. With keeping the margins high, there are low chances of latency which you can expect over the period of time. The time rate will be able to keep the support on the assistance of customer, account manager and the subscription fee which is there for the charges also available over the period of time. The support will be there for the assistance and for the matter of fact, you can keep the customer success on high rate as well.

5.1.11 Trading on High Frequency

The frequency of trading within Cobinhood is always high with keeping the subscription level on the services. The networks work over the funds which are investors for many and hosts the services over exchanges. You have to keep the engines on the ticker latency aong with keeping the API rate in control. The servers keep track of the algorithms with knowing that the trading will be working over the fee of subscription which has no additional cost to it.

5.1.12 Underwriting Services

Keeping the underwriting services of ICO under consideration, you can keep the launch of the fee easily perfect on you rend.

5.1.13 Financial Aspect

Another importance factor can be the indexes in the market along with the services which are produced as the centers are able to launch within the products. The wallet and the services which are there for the help of the cryptocurrencies will be able to keep the products easily finances throughout. Keeping the Cobinhood high quality services will be done through the wallet and easy payments throughout as well.

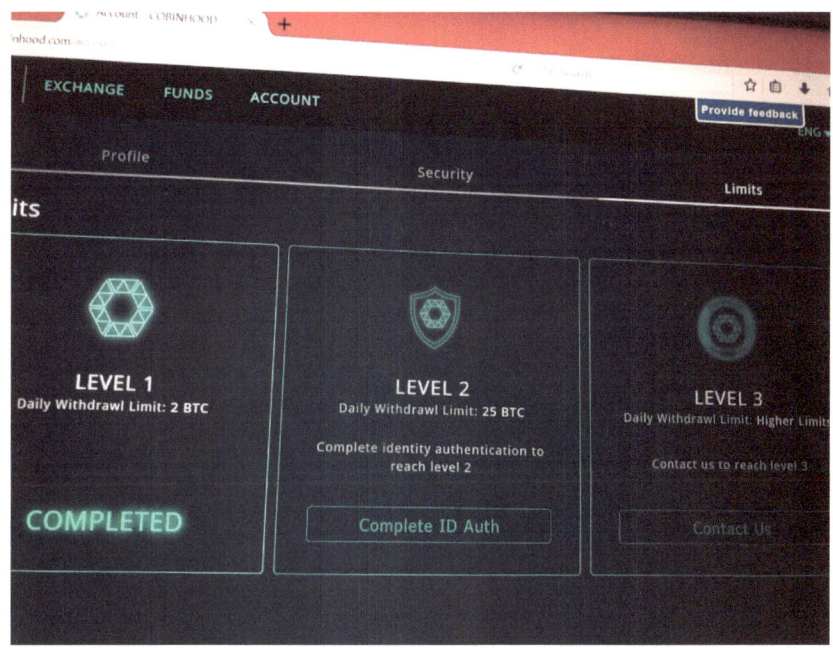

5.2 Dexon and Cobinhood

One of the biggest crypto exchange is known as Cobinhood according to the records. It is 11th largest exchange with having the launch of Dexon which is the platform for it. The platform of Dexon is centralized with having no fee attached to it. It is based upon the blockchain technology with having ventures and capitals attached to it. There is entire management which is based over the platform and works fast.

There are bankers, investors and other fund raises included in the transactions of Dexon. The structure of Dexon helps in the transactions which are decentralized and scalable to measure as well. It helps in releasing the states quickly with having various features attached to it. There are many systems which work on one platform of Dexon and easy to manage. It helps in keeping the implementation of blockchain technology on prior basis.

Upon the initial stages of blockchain, the CEO of Dexon wants to avail all the benefits for running it smoothly. The influence of the industry is emerging and there are ecosystems which are being applied. It helps in measuring the structure with keeping the system together in the parallel way out. The transactions and the speed is commendable when it comes to Dexon. The network of Dexon will be able to compete with the high tech companies with using the most convenient way of attempting the financial transactions online.

The cryptocurrency service of Cobinhood has been providing the trading and underwriting of ICO generally. The aim is to sort out the problems with the exchanges between the cryptocurrency exchanges. There are no trading fees which are associated with the market and the profit of the liquidated value of Cobinhood.

The processing and its ability takes up to more than half a second with accessing the experience of trading online. It performs in high frequency with knowing that the trading options have the issues to get resolved with the underwriting of the service which is over the issues to be maintained with Cobinhood.

BTC BCC ETH ETC

LTC ZEC XMR XRP

COB NEO OMG USDT

DASH IOTA EOS REP GNT

Chapter 6: JOYSO

JOYSO is an Ethereum based exchange that offers the speed of a centralized platform while offering the privacy and security of one decentralized exchange. You have to accept this contract before using this exchange.

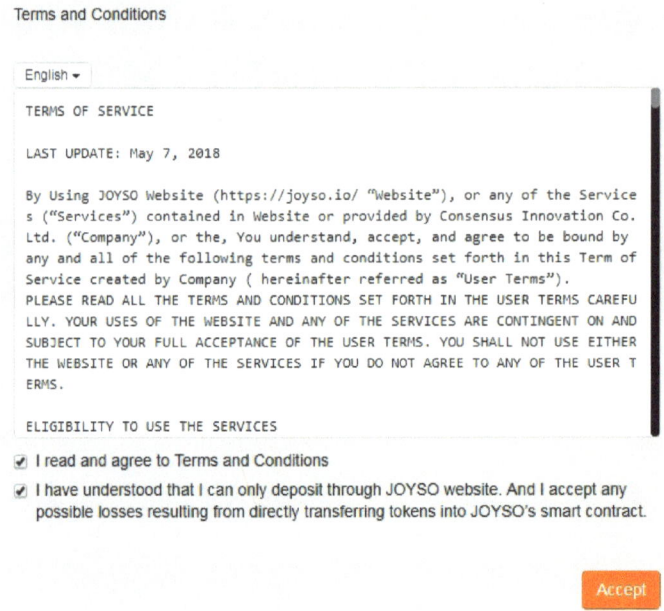

6.1 How does this exchange work?

6.1.1 Deposit for JOYSO

Before you start trading, deposit cryptocurrencies to a JOYSO exchange. This exchange will not hold cryptocurrencies and acts as a bridge to assist your trade.

6.1.2 Matching on the Platform

Once you place a trade, matching system of JOYSO activates and match your real time orders.

6.1.3 Confirmation on Blockchain

After matching an order, all successfully matched orders are placed on blockchain Ethereum. Computers in the world will work to confirm your orders.

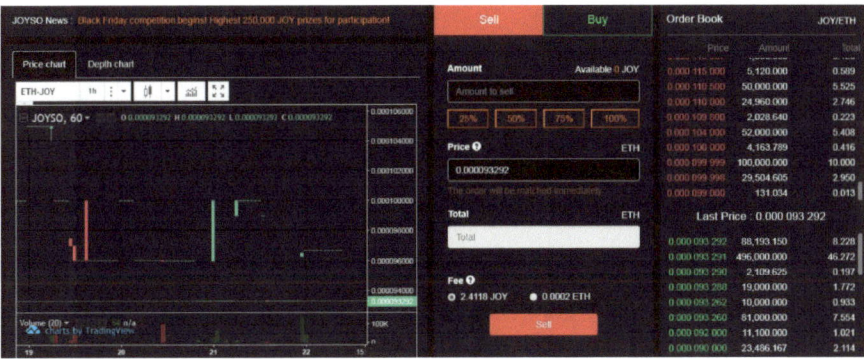

6.2 Features of JOYSO

- **Smart Match:** It is off-chain smart matching to efficiently match the orders.
- **Lower Fees:** Charges of gas are lower than decentralized exchanges.
- **Transparent:** The trades are transparent on blockchain with maximum transparency.
- **Smart Contract:** JOYO can't directly alter the account balance of user.

JOYSO is known as the token which is used as the hybrid trading in cryptocurrency. The exchange is based on centralization with having various features attached to it. The privacy and the security has been improved by JOYSO due to which it is more trustable now. The HEX (Hybrid Exchange) works with compatibility of the tokens which are easy to handle. It takes away the exchange which is based centrally with having the information privately and keeping the minimal history to avoid any mislead event.

The key helps in being the protection of all the personal information which can eliminate the risk of hacking. The chain of order taking works with having the prices which are compared through multiple innovations. There are many benefits which are attached with JOYSO such as it helps in the order limits with having the reasonable price of the tokens.

The chain and the matchings process with having fast pace over the smart machines. The issues of security of any arbitrage is handled by the smart machines which are reliable too. It is easy to run multiple transactions with JOYSO without any error. It helps in merging the orders with having exchanges which are decentralized. The alternation in the account needs to be balanced with the user. At the same time, the assets of the users are not allowed for them to view when they have made the trade.

It still needs to go through the signing up process with JOYSO but the users are able to directly use the smart contract with bidding on the wallet easily. They have the access to cancel any transaction which they want unless it is not matched. The accessibility to have the lock for smart contracts is also available with JOYSO.

The trades which get published with the user needs to have the transparency for anyone to purchase them on this platform. It is also traceable if you would like to avail that option. Among all the other platforms, JOYSO is one platform which is cost effective along with multiple features to it.

The cost of settlement and the transaction low users are also keeping the structure aligned with it.

6.3 Difference between Decentralized and Centralized Exchange

As JOYSO is equipped with multiple features, there are two exchanges which occur in it. The decentralized exchange and the centralized exchange. Let's look into the briefing of each to understand the difference of both.

6.3.1 Decentralized Exchange

The decentralized exchange does not depend upon any service of third party for the funds of the customers. The trading between the users is done directly without any third party being involved. The process is automated which let the users interact with each other with complete anonymity. The tokens are achieved through the proxy or the assets over the escrow system. It is done through the signature with having the solutions provided instantly as well. The list may include blackhalo, blocket, bitsquare and Coinffeine. It helps in controlling the funds of the customers as well as remaining anonymous. There is no risk of any hacker tracing your information because of the ultimate security with the platform.

You do not have to submit any person documents for the registration on this platform. There is no fee applied for trading as well. Whereas, it can take some time to learn about the platform and the features. As the acquaintance increases, the features tend to get easier for the user. If the hacker is successful at hacking your computer then there is no chance of surviving within this platform which is the biggest flaw of it so far.

6.3.2 Centralized Exchange

This exchange is also known as the traditional exchange between the users. There is one main website where the users are trading and making their transactions for cryptocurrencies. It helps in trading the currencies like BTC, ripple and more. The list may include simplefx, poloniex, CEX and more.

There are more advanced features in the exchange which are easy to use for the users. They are self-explanatory so there is no training required to it. The more user spends time on it, the more chances to learn it completely and quickly. The tools are advance with having the liquidity of adaption fast. There is a control over the funds with the centralized exchange. The requirement is there for the personal documents which need to be submitted. There can be a time for the website can be down or may have been attacked by the hacker. It is not anonymous so you the person you would be trading with would be knowing your name for sure.

6.3.3 Why is JOYSO called a mixed exchange?

The main reason for JOYSO being the mixed exchange is because it provides you two options for exchanges. The traditional way of centralization and then the decentralization. Both have their pros and cons which you have to accept when you are signing up with this platform. It is easy to use but the complication may depend upon the exchange type which you choose.

It gives you multiple options within one exchange and you do have the choice to switch to another if you are not satisfied with one. You have to make the deposits with JOYSO so that you are able to continue the trading with it. It helps you finding the right and the smart match which is beneficial for your accounts. The fees are lower and you are able to work with in the best way. There is nothing hidden in the trades which is why you have to be transparent on your end. There cannot be any alteration within the process of smart contracts so make sure that you are aware of all these facts before you start off with JOYSO.

6.4 Services of JOYSO

6.4.1 Explaining CEX, DEX and HEX

The efficiency of CEX, DEX and HEX has been comparatively faster than other cryptocurrencies under the JOYSO. There are some of the vulnerable aspects to keep in mind when you are working with JOYSO and its components. The management tends to be over the losses which is there for the exchanges along with keeping the trading easy. The investors work over the losses and the companies make a forward move of keeping decentralization.

With having the exchanges of DEX, you will be able to get the experience which would be pretty satisfying throughout the process. There are limited orders which get processed under DEX whereas, it is not the same for CEX. The architecture keeps on moving rapidly with keeping the blockchain and its associates under considerations.

Having the efficiency of the products, there are some of the fees which are based on transactions. You have to keep the convenience on your end with defining the main goals of being in the blockchain services. Keeping the traders and the nodes under the line, the processing system should be defined lately within time frame.

The process should be done without any manipulation of the terms along with keeping the modifications under the line. You have to keep the traders and the market aligned with the latency and terms which need to be on time as well. Having the right information is necessary in the matter of HEX along with keeping smooth interactions within the blockchain platform.

6.5 Architecture of JOYSO

With the architecture of JOYSO which is hybrid and works with the speed of transactions, there are some of the matchings which you have to consider in order to keep it aligned. The security works with keeping the processes aligned and there are some of the stocks which can be functional for you. The limitations of the processes will be sending the instructions which are based on the orders and deposits by JOYSO. You will have to keep the signs within the tokens to keep the interface friendly for the users.

The prices are possibly best with JOYSO as you work along with keeping the benefits in mind. The off the chain working with the blockchain can be easily found with matching the sources of the smart contracts. You have to keep the changes which are visible to the users so they are able to access it and modify them accordingly to their own requirements which they want to construct on the online platform.

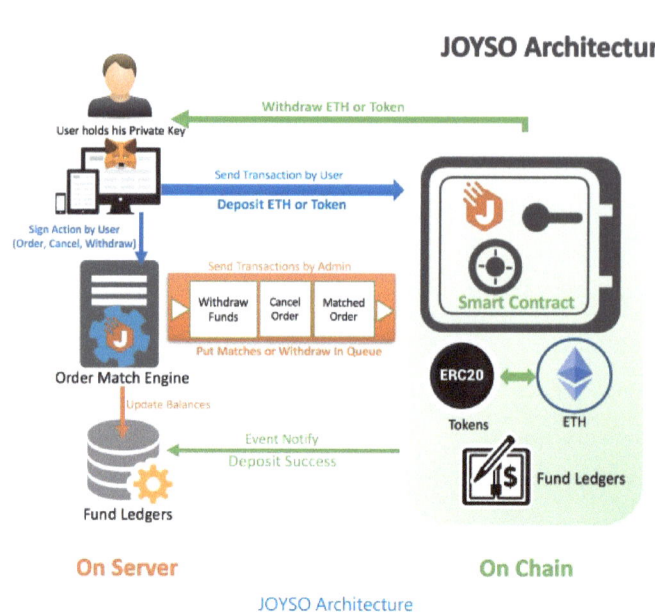

JOYSO Architecture

6.6 ICO Market for JOYSO

The market of ICO has been raised for JOYSO in the past few months due to which you have to keep the transactions wisely on the market. The challenges are there which will be met over the extensions for bitcoins when meeting with the tokens of JOYSO.

You have to make sure to keep the exchanges as the time passes with keeping the plans of tokens aligned with ERC20 tokens which can be easily worked out. The simple process of the ICOs are there to be formed when there are situations which you have to present as the time passes.

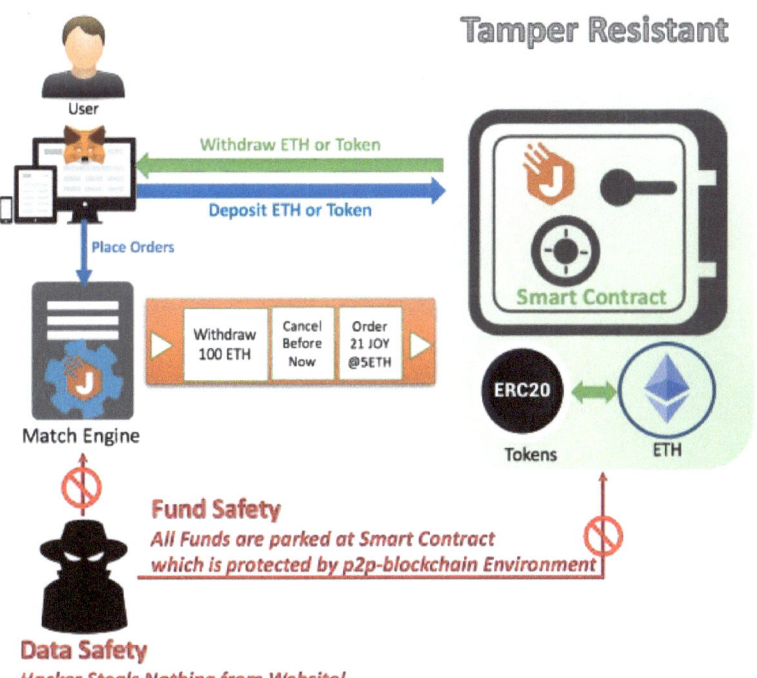

Keeping the transactions at place, there are some of the factors which you have to trade between the time and costs to keep it sensible for the users. You will not have to keep the repetition processes so that the experience is smooth with the clients who are using the information and working out with it through the extensions.

6.7 Competition with JOYSO

There is a lot of competition which works around JOYSO and can be proven in order to get great deals out of it. The advantages can get through the benefits which are hybrid and able to pay off with the ability of sharing with the competition. The market shows solutions which are focused on having the centralized exchanges possible for the accuracy over the market.

When you have principals defined within the market, there are less chances that you would require any changes within the segments. Keeping in mind that the competition with Ether

Delta works within the money transfer and trades which occur over the blockchain platform easily.

There are more than million orders which occur for the encryption of the orders keeping the accounts active through Ether Delta. Lately, there has been a lot of private key stealing on the Ether Delta which proves to make it an unreliable platform to work with. The company has apologized publicly with keeping the books in order to maintain the privacy of the users and making sure to make it stronger.

On the other side, the 0xProtocol works throughout the exchange without settling as the server to hand over the books. The decentralized project works with the pool of keeping the liquidated amount of time within the exchanges.

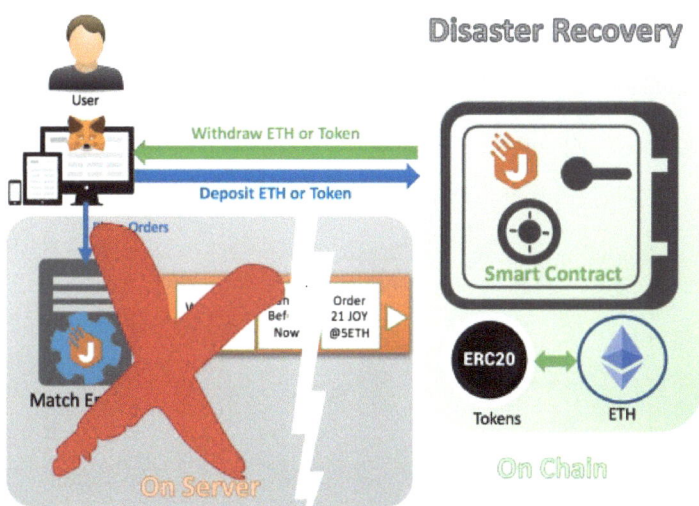

**Even if the disaster occurs on server,
User still Can Withdraw from Smart Contract Directly**

The value of the tokens get increased within the passing time when it is operation through 0xprotocol and you have to keep the regular positing within the fees of charges. Having the people find the right execution in the market, you can keep the orders in the right way of working with conventional services.

With the swapping protocols, you can keep the lines interesting and working within the processes to make sure that price is there for the right orders of JOYSO and its limitations are followed well too.

6.8 Business Model

The business model works through keeping the effective tokens of JOYSO aligned within the makers of percentages. Having the transactions and its generations, there are some of the frictions which you can mention as you work along the profits of the tokens. The announcements over the parts of JOYSO will help you leave the phases of trading which gets used with the comparative part of the exchanges.

You have to keep the tokens aligned with keeping the measurements of the discounts which are offered to the clients with getting the right information on track. The profits will be able to generate through the advertisements which are found on JOYSO tokens and work out equally on the part of keeping the reduction plans.

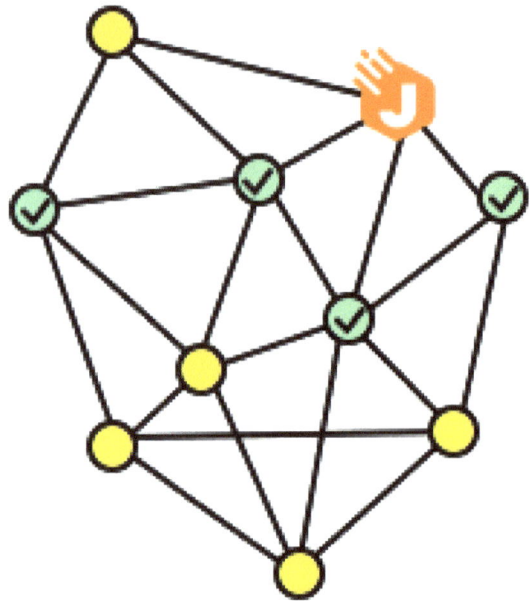

With the listings which are there for your effort to keep the trading on the cost of operations, you will be able to offer the right job for the community. Along with the set of features which you can work through, there will be associations which can keep the arguments on the zipped manner without any consumptions of the settlement costs. When you have integration over the community, you will be likely to gain experience within the market as the time passes for the tokens to keep a usage of ultimate outcome which you can use for a long time.

Measure the phase which is upcoming and keep the decentralized systems aligned in order to make sure that you have the consensus to meet in order to keep the rights reserved. With knowing the information of the systems, you can work over the expensive costs of settlements which are there for the community and blockchain are able to reduce the wallets and integration over the course of time.

6.9 Marketing Planning

For JOYSO, marketing planning has to work accurately in order to have the survival in the market. The digital currency works between the ages of 26-36 for the people who are interested to invest smarter with keeping many opportunities under the line. The markets show over the security and the networks work throughout the trading options of the speed.

Keeping the hybrid exchange of JOYSO under consideration, there are some of the features of marketing plan which you need to keep in mind when working throughout. The plan has to work with the funds which you control first. There are private keys which you have to work with otherwise, you will not be able to access the information throughout the learning phase of this product.

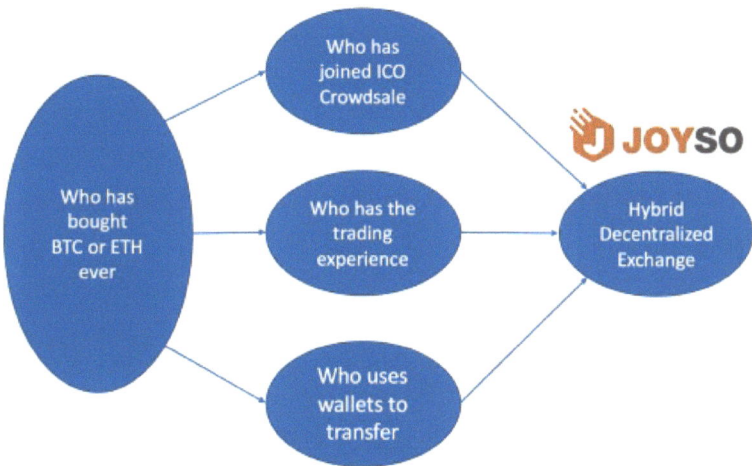

Target Audience:
Market segmentation and the user experience journey

With having the centralization along with HEX, you can keep the markets simple within one language which is easy to understand by all. The powerful ICO investments are done by the Chinese so if you wish to add the language within the course, that would be convenient for the media to keep the trading simple and easy to expect within the market.

The advice over the marketing plan would be to keep the marketing program comprehensives over the period of time so you are able to plan the campaign easily as well. Keeping the advantages under control with languages which are easy to read and build over the period of time. The content of the page needs to be strong so it retains the users with the information which is required to keep the adoption of the ICOs. The artwork, written content, videos and much more can keep the page interesting and engaging for the users to hold on to within the pattern of the time knowing that what they have to initiate in Taiwan for the blockchain of JOYSO and how to follows its compatible pattern along as well.

Usage of social channels can prove to be powerful tool to prepare the marketing plan for JOYSO as it builds up the conferences and gatherings online. You will be able to prepare the right costs of keeping the decentralized systems along with knowing the lower aspects of blockchain as well. The tokens which are accessed by JOYSO will be there for you to keep the profile high and build it even stronger over the period of time.

The panels work through the networks which can bring out the valuable information with having the appearances to deal with. You can keep the events in the plans knowing that channels will be promoting over the engagements of gatherings online and events which are there for the advantage of the tokens presented to the people who are involved in the implementation of this plan easily.

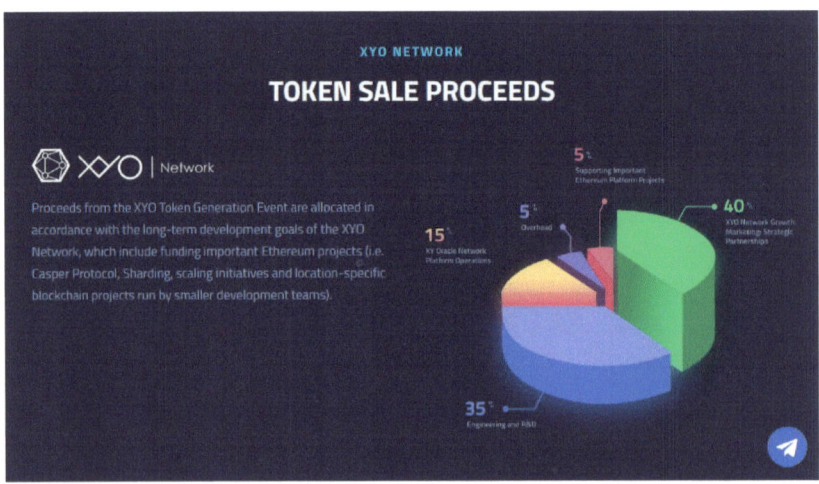

Chapter 7: STAR BIT

7.1 0x protocol and ZRX

0X is a protocol with a messaging system where people build the transactions online. The 0x protocol and ZRX is the future which everyone is looking up to. 0x protocol works as a training for anything which is done on the blockchain and not just focusing on the tokens. Earlier it was a protocol which was built for the ethereum blockchain. The off chain commands where signed in with the help of private key which is assigned to each user on blockchain. The broadcasts are done with letting the users find their counterparties easily. The orders are easily found for the people upon their wish and the type of the orders they are looking for on the blockchain. The verification is done through the signature of the tokens and they are swapped between two parties.

The order book is able to take the notes with having the submission at that same time. The orders are done directly with keeping the nodes together of ethereum and it does not need any permission. The centralized system matches the requirements and then the collisions of trading are done. The providers give you the open for the quotes and you have to reserve them in order to proceed for the later references. Other options of 0x protocol and ZRX can be related to the derivatives relayers, auctions and dark pools.

The non-fungible tokens have been changed in the new version of 0x protocol 2.0 which has arisen of Cryptokitties and Cryptopunks. The popularity of these have increased over the period of time. The collections of games and instruments of finances have been presented earlier with 0x protocols.

Another thing to consider with the new version is the compliance of regulations. The companies are finding the framework easier on the blockchain. Big companies are working within the network to get through the compliances. The types of assets which are mentioned on blockchain tends to have the integration easily now. There are various schemes which have been offered to find out about the flexibility of transactions and the security along with it.

The filtration of smart contracts allow you to have the smooth integration within blockchain platform. It helps the developers to have the addition of smart contracts which can be performed as the routed way of getting the ideas through. The pools are there in the liquidated form with having the ideas enabled and permissions are granted too.

There is enforcement on the side to keep the routing aligned. The trading functions perform well with keeping the matching orders with the blockchain nature and functions. You will be able to take complete advantage of this protocol as it keeps on getting advanced and you will be working with the trading options in everything but not just the tokens.

According to the market of capital and coins, the capitalization works through the assets which are present in blockchain. Star Bit is one of the popular and increasing bitcoin which has been availed by the users within one or more year. The volume of trading has increased rapidly with keeping the exchanges in the possible value and working through revenues as the time passed.

The introduction of this bitcoin has the ledger which maintains all the information about the transactions which occur on Star Bit. According to the development and its working transparency on the internet, the technologies have gained huge popularity.

The lawmakers work through the processes to make it simple for the businesses to handle over the payments and their verification systems. When there is huge development within the processes, you will be able to find globally available currencies which serves to be one of the attitudes you can acquire with keeping the smooth connections with generating daily revenues.

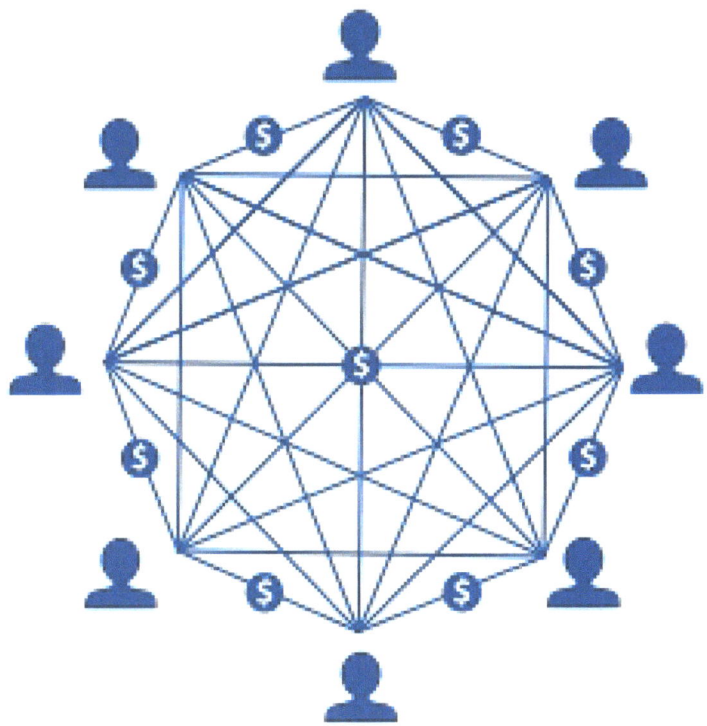

The development of the blockchain technology works over the regulations which are there for the settlement act and the regulations are being followed. The currencies work over the executions which are not known for any applications and sustained as the time passes. You will be able to make the attitudes sustained within the countries which are positive about blockchain and support the cause of trading assets in order to make money out of it.

7.2 Services with Star Bit

The demand for Star Bit increased in 2013 with the investors in the blockchain platform. As it was the start, it took the rise with having the exchanges based on centralization only. The third part could not access the system within the buyers or the sellers. The personal information was maintained until the centralized system and only one server would be receiving the information in the following keeping of the security lines. To prevent form the main information, the exchanges worked out the customers through assets which are digitally through the security measurements.

Having the transactions within the bitcoin, the servers got hacked and lately it has been fixed coming back to the revival so that people are able to invest in it to make more money out it. The structure has changed with keeping the exchanges with preventing any attack on the server so the customers can keep the work aligned. The values and the prices changed the cryptocurrencies with keeping result evitable strong on the end of the sellers and the buyers.

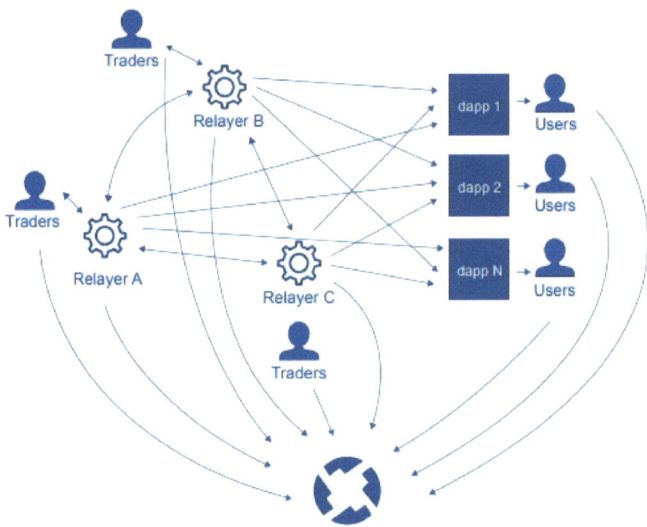

7.3 Decentralized Challenges: EtherDelta, 0x Protocol

The developers are able to work through the principles which are there to keep the platform simply available for the tokens. When the architecture has been shown on the smart contracts, they worked through the Ether delta which is similar to keep the assets secured on the web. The exchanges done on the tokens are required by the clients which are there for the rate of transactions and their low access of information. The combining trades work through solutions which can be there for the user experience and their enhancements so you can easily work out with it.

CENTRALIZED   DECENTRALIZED

BINANCE
BITFINEX
POLONIEX

kyber network
EtherDelta
0x Protocol

The 0xProtocol has the source which is open and regulated over the peer to peer connection. The system of tokens is different with it keeping the development of the technologies aligned with the teams of professionals. You can keep the forecasts of the platforms aligned with developing various applications for the 0xprotocol.

7.4 Principles of Star Bit

With the help of smart contracts, it has been easier for the Star Bit to form principles to keep the services engaging for the users. When there are blockchain which are decentralized and working over the codes of programs, it becomes a smooth process.

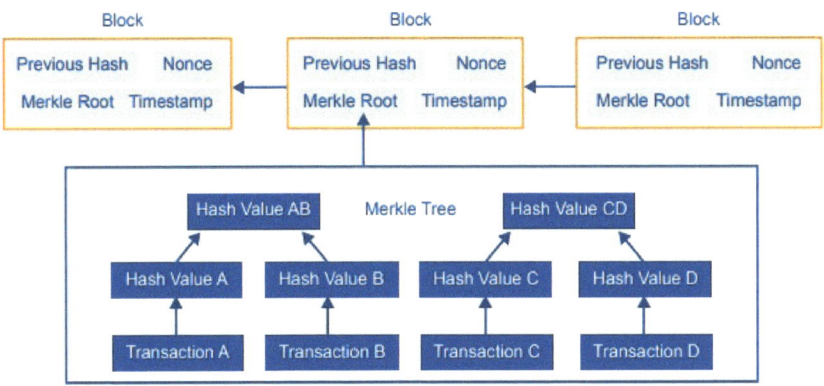

(Fig. 1-4) Architecture of the smart contract

The information being shared works with keeping the payment of the tokens through other information which can be recorded on the basis of the technologies and their working hours. The impact becomes through the market and has a strong impression of keeping the work aligned with matching their processes. The proof works with the team and there are transaction history which is required to look into the accounts when you are working with Star Bit.

There can be problems which you would face but you have to be efficient and tasks can be reliable with matching orders. The information should be secure and safe to use for the access of ledger which maintains over the period of time.

7.5 Star Wallet

Another important aspect of Star Bit is the star wallet which is easy to use and understand by the users. It can be used as an application which has the open source of working through the projects of tokens with Star Bit. The safe and secure system of Star Bit wallet allows you to work through the interface which is friendly and smooth to operate. The private key gives you the complete protection of accessing your account without the involvement of any third party.

As long as you keep the private key safe, your assets and transactions will be safe. There is a code of memory which you can provide to keep the maintenance of the wallet along with the applications which are interfaced through the protection and users. You have to keep the measurements under considerations and work through estimated processes with accessing the wallet once in a while to check on the progress. To keep it active, it is better to sign in once a day in order to check and keep track of all the regulated information of the account.

7.6 Token Offerings – Star Bit Token

The tokens which are offered by Star Bit works through the generations of the digital blockchain technology. Having the volume of legal currency, there are tokens which are standard and officially maintained. The smart contracts which are there for the management would ensure the tokens to be on the future and have no additional cost to it. With the high offerings, the maintenance charges will be there for the holders to keep the handling of the maintenance on the hold. The smart contracts are there for the currency along with keeping the proportions within the matter of time.

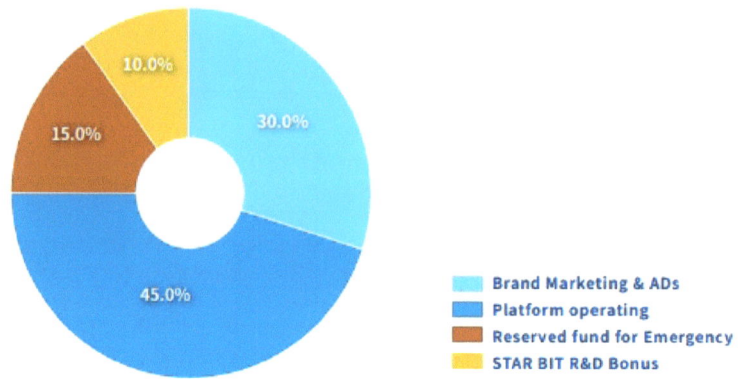

Star Bit is able to continue within the proportion of time where the rate of feasibility is high and works through the tokens easily. When you have the orders maintained as the pool of largest section, the world will require the maintenance over the trends. The distributions are there up to 30% of the times which are calculated as the address of each user may differ. You have to keep the dividends high to make sure that the corresponding address can make full usage of the tokens easily. The 0xprotocol works with keeping the exchanges centralized as the transactions processed over time.

The investors are able to make it hard to work through it and with the help of satisfactory results, you will be able to find the relevant data online within next time. The dividends allow you to keep the monthly investments aside when you are working through the Star Bit tokens.

Chapter 8: Conclusion

Crypto exchanges facilitate traders to trade coins, tokens and digital assets. You can find out things about the status of cryptocurrency in Taiwan. Understand the rules and regulations that can change the life of traders interested in digital currency.

Acknowledgement

- Jo-Yu Duh
- Wei-Shiun Chen

www.ingramcontent.com/pod-product-compliance
Lightning Source LLC
Chambersburg PA
CBHW040322220526
45473CB00009B/2534